I0165137

Also by Sarah Elle Emm

LAST VACATION

NACREOUS
Harmony Run Series, Book 4

CHATOYANT,
Harmony Run Series, Book 3

OPALESCENT,
Harmony Run Series, Book 2

PRISMATIC,
Harmony Run Series, Book 1

MARRYING MISSY

Absence of You

A collection of poems

by

Sarah Elle Emm

Next Chapter Media

Absence of You is a work of fiction. Names, characters, places, and incidents either are products of the author's imagination or are used fictitiously. This work is protected in full by all applicable copyright laws, as well as by misappropriation, trade secret, unfair competition, and other applicable laws. No part of this book may be used or reproduced in any manner whatsoever without written permission from the author, except in the case of brief quotations embodied in critical articles and reviews. All rights reserved.

Absence of You
Copyright © 2016 by Sarah Elle Emm

Next Chapter Media, LLC.

www.SarahElleEmm.com

Cover design by Natasha Brown
Typesetting by Odyssey Books
Author Photo by Brand Photo Design

ISBN: 978-0-692-70062-4

Published in the United States of America

In loving memory of my Grandpa Doc,

How I miss you. Everything…your hugs, your jokes, your smile. And I miss reading your comments on my poetry blogs. We'll meet again, Abuelo.

~Sarita

Praise for Sarah Elle Emm's poetry from her readers:

"There is a gentleness about Sarah's writings." ~Mischa

"Beautiful!" ~Maria

"Sarah's poems touch my heart." ~Rohini

"Heartfelt!" ~Francis

"I love everything she writes." ~ Aaron

"Love the way she scatters words!" ~Amber

"Sarah's poetry speaks to my heart." ~Sharon

"Wow!" ~Janet

"Her poems pierce through the heart." ~Jade

"Soulful!" ~Raj

"Touched my heart and fuels my writer's soul." ~Jacquelyn

"Tragically beautiful." ~ Andrea

For my readers

From the bottom of my heart, thank you for taking this journey with me. You are a tremendous blessing.

Contents

I

Fallen

Before A Sound

Before a sound was uttered
From lips I'd know in time
Before hands touched,
Names exchanged
You laid it on the line

From across a crowded room
You gave your heart to mine
Before we'd even met,
You told me with your eyes.

Tidal Wave

I wasn't prepared for the surge
And honestly neither were you,
We couldn't have foreseen the undertow
Or known we might not make it through

As the forces swept us straight under
We clung to each other so tight,
Not knowing or caring if the tide would let up
Or if we would even survive

I wasn't prepared for the currents
I wasn't prepared for the fall,
But for the tidal wave of our love, ups and downs,
I would still cling to you; I'd risk it all.

Shameless

I was in a box
A convenience
A tool for the occasional need,
No one saw me completely
Or wanted more than just fragments of me

But in one instant
You saw my value
I saw it happen, your gaze settled on me
I'd be yours, not partially,
But fully
You were shamelessly devoted to all of me.

First Kiss

You told me how long
You'd waited for me,
You told me how I'd
Been the missing piece
You told me a tale
Of a long-awaited wish,
You said so many words
In our very first kiss.

Love Note

I ran my fingers
Across the letters
My cheeks heated
As my skin swept the ink,
Wondering how something so simple
Could push my emotions
So near the brink

I traced your words
With my fingertips
Each syllable
I caressed,
Your love note left me mesmerized,
I'm taken, I confess.

Manic State

Manic state
Each breath that escapes
You possess these thoughts
Asleep or awake

I was sound before
Sweet ignorant bliss
But how circumstances changed
With the brush of your lips.

Love in the Way

I was waiting
Till the time was right
I was climbing
Up the ladder,
Knees getting weak
Was for the rest of them
Staying focused
Was all that mattered

Till one day
I was racing along
When you refused to let me pass,
My knees began to buckle
As you took my hand,
List, ladder forgotten,
Just like that.

Letter

Here I am,
Penning a letter
The ink is my heart pounding for you,
If I confess
Put it on record
Perhaps this fervency
Will begin to unglue

Though I fight against the pull
You're clearly my drug
I don't know what to do,
So I'll put it all in writing
In hopes it will be a cure for you

Here I am
Penning this letter
The ink is my heart pounding for you,
Trying to put into words this craze,
This insane
Addiction
To you.

Music

Your eyes summoned my heart
To play it's true song,
The irregular beat of before
Was forgotten, it had been wrong

Your eyes summoned my heart
To play an authentic melody,
To flutter in time with it's fated match
In flawless harmony

Your eyes summoned my heart
To respond to you alone,
And now it races with a fierceness,
An intensity I'd never known

Your eyes summoned my heart
To match the momentum of your song,
It recognized your music
And is finally at home, where it belongs.

Fool

You made a fool of yourself for me
With the earnest note you read aloud,
Amidst a crowd, eavesdropping
You spoke your words,
You spelled it out

With the slightest tremble in your movement,
You reached across the table for me,
You took my hand, your voice unwavering
Declared your love for me

There was never any qualm
How to respond to your declaration,
Though others had spoken those candid words,
Professed their admiration

I had never known how compelling
A note and the shortest phrase could be,
But suddenly you spoke three words
Made a fool of yourself for me

You made a fool of yourself for me
I knew exactly what to do,
I replied, "I know. And I love you."
I made a fool of myself for you.

Immune

The seconds can pass
Turn into hours
The sky could erupt
In meteor showers

The people can talk
I don't hear a sound
My feet could be walking
On shifting ground

The worries, the list,
The pain from before
I've forgotten it all
I feel so secure

My smile won't fade
As rain starts to fall
When you hold my hand
I'm immune to it all.

Blind Hands

You touch me with hands
Blind to imperfection
Whispering praise
As they trail my skin,
Offering affection
Blind hands that overpower
Insecurities and doubt
Blind hands that rescue me
From demons hiding out
Blind hands that fill my lungs
With soothing, steady breath
So hold me in your healing arms,
Blind hands, make me forget.

Home

I had nothing to explain
I didn't have to justify,
You accepted me for who I was
You never batted an eye

There was nothing I needed to fix
Nothing I needed to change,
To you I was perfection
Hearing the words felt unreal, strange

Being myself was easy
There was freedom I'd longed to know,
You loved me without questions, conditions
Refused to let me go

I didn't need to run
For once I'd found a home,
I was safe in your arms, unconditionally yours
I didn't have to go it alone.

Save Your Words

Save your words
Use your arms
To tell me what
I need to hear

Save your words
Your heart is speaking
As it beats against my ear

Save your words
Talk with hands
It's the moment's cure-all pill

Save your words
For when I need them
Because eventually, I will.

II

Broken

Somewhere Between

We watched them fall apart
With words they couldn't take back,
From across the restaurant hand in hand
Swore we'd never be like that

Huddled in the booth
We cringed at their spiteful tones,
Right then and there they ended it
Said they were better off alone

We hated the space between them
But somewhere between then and now,
There's a gap too large to close
We became that couple,
We forgot our vow.

Waiting

I waited for you
In our usual place
I searched the crowd
For the only face
That could ease this pain
At merely the sight
Yet temp and torment
My dreams each night
I stayed past the hour
Of our regular meet
Now my symptoms are worse
You weren't waiting for me.

Bled onto Pages

I bled onto pages
To spare you the grief
I was holding inside,
Blood mixed with my tears, my ink
Wove a desperate tale of another time,
As pages climbed towards the sky
The burn in my chest
Began to subside,
Till the pain lie dormant once more
And the blood, ink, and tears
Had nearly run dry.

Reach

Reach for me
Spare me
The slightest brush
Of shoulders
In passing,
Like a breeze
With it's subtle caress,
And I'll know
There's hope for us yet.

Call Me Pretty

Call me pretty
Tell me lies,
However I change
You'll be by my side

Tell me it's the way I think
That makes your pulse race wild for me,
Tell me it's the words I say
That draw you close, make you glance my way

Forget my face, the feel of my skin
The curve of my hips didn't pull you in,
Tell me it was a feeling inside
Your heart had found a match for the very first time

Tell me how you love my soul
More than a body that's growing old,
Fool me, make me believe it's true
Tell me I'm more than a doll to you

Don't call me pretty
Forget the lies,
Whatever keeps you drawn,
I'm here, by your side.

Shut out

When you shut me out of your circle,
You broke the thread connecting us,
I stood in the dimness, aghast, alone,
No one left to trust

It nearly broke my spirit
Watching you throw my love away,
I tried to get back in
Travailed till there was nothing left to say

When you shut me out of your circle
I had a decision to make,
Though it hurt in the gloom of your circle,
I found the strength so I could stay.

Turn Around

Turn around
Give me a chance
To offer the words
You need to hear,
Turn around
I won't choke on each sound
I'll let go of pride
Each note will be clear

Turn around
Before courage dwindles
I'll say anything
Ignore doubts and fears,
Turn around
Just give me this chance
To offer the syllables
That will keep you right here.

Leave

Leave again
If that's what it takes
To make you miss me
If it's the action
That will bring you
Back to me
If that's how your heart notices
The expanse between us

If leaving means
You'll say the words
I haven't heard for so long,
If it means I'll find myself in
Your embrace on your return,
Leave again
Leave,
Be gone.

I Can

I can't take away your pain
Or quiet the villains in your mind,
But I can listen, comfort, and hold
I can be here by your side

I can't erase the things that haunt you
Or even imagine how you hurt inside
But I can be here, listening, holding
I can be here by your side.

Carefree Corner

Meet me on the corner
Where flowers tumble from boxes,
Shops gleam in afternoon rays,
I'll take your hand and stroll
We'll ignore instincts to escape

The sun will smooth my worry lines
For a moment I'll be carefree,
And maybe you will see me
The way that you love me

We'll only stroll a little while
The world won't let us be free,
Still, meet me,
Meet me on the corner
And for a little while we'll dream.

No Words Required

You said your part
And I said mine,
We stand opposed
A divided line

The signs are there
It's the end of us,
We've burned each other
Destroyed the trust

Yet here we stand
Unwilling to move,
This stare down
Neither wants to lose

So save your voice
Fight has made me tired,
I'll meet you in the middle
No words required.

Drug I Can't Quit

The drug I can't quit
Self-hate
And regret
I knew when we met
You'd burn what was left
Of pieces of me
Barely clinging together
I can't blame you for the pain,
The destruction, or clatter
Though the remnants of my soul
Are dissolving to bits
You're the drug I won't quit,
I deserve all of this.

Sorry

I wanted you to know
I was sorry
For the words
That sparked our demise,
But by the time
I worked up the courage
You were gazing
Into her eyes.

Conquest

If I was just a conquest to you,
Why did you take my hand?
Why did you push me to the point of no return,
If I wasn't part of your plan?

If I wasn't the girl of your dreams,
Not the other half of your heart,
Why did you tell me you loved me
And make me devoted to you from the start?

If I was just a conquest to you,
It's my fault, I should have seen,
But your whisper, your lies, they covered my eyes
And I let myself fall for the dream.

Missing Parts

When you packed your bags,
You took the part of me that still believed
In first glances stopping time and space,
That treasured the crossing of paths
And undeniable fate.
I've searched the empty drawers
And this hollow shell of a heart,
But no matter how much I search
I can't find my missing parts.

To Your Liking

Let your fingers trail my arms
In a lingering goodbye,
Simply a moment before you run to your world,
A few seconds of your time

As they settle on my wrist
Blaze a trail across my skin,
I imagine I'll still be to your liking
By the time you walk through the door again.

Insanity

I walk the dim-lit space
Wondering where you go at night,
As if each step might lead me closer
To the peace I long to find

I will the thoughts to stop
But insanity rules the night,
I pause to write down the words
That are piercing my mind like a knife

Unable to rest in the silence
I wonder how to get through, what to do,
I imagine a world where you want me beside you
Where I'm free from this sting of solitude

Write, pace, write, pace
Until I've worn the carpet and my mind,
I'm exhausted; I surrender to sleep for now
It's yours; You can have the night.

Muddling

We both suffer
Our own sicknesses
Have needs
That are rarely met,
Yet here we stand
In this same room
Still muddling
Through the mess.

Clinging

I'm clinging to this raft
Holding on for life
But my fortitude is dwindling
I'm fighting, griping the line

And unexpectedly you're here,
All of my hope returns
But then you shift,
Sealing our death,
I'm whisked away in the torrid currents.

Your Shadows

It's frigid in the shadows
But here I'll stand on quivering legs,
Praying for strength and courage
As your light gets further away

If one day the glare isn't blinding you,
Your eyes open, and you might know,
I merely wanted to bask in the beams
You shine wherever you go,

I never tried to steal
The artificial lights as they rained down on you,
I only wanted to feel the warmth of your rays,
A particle or two…

I'm in the darkness, your light is diminishing, fading,
I can't stop shivering,
But here I'll stand, as long as my legs will hold me,
Until shadows have devoured the last of me.

Vile Words

Even as I spoke those vile words,
Aimed like poison-tipped arrows at your heart,
I wanted you to refute them
I wanted you to prove me wrong,
But now the hope that you'll fight for me
It continues to fade, is nearly gone

And the poison-tipped arrows came back to me
They plunged into my core
Those vile words ceaselessly haunt me
In the unconscious and awake,
I wanted you to prove me wrong
But I fear it might be too late.

Eruption

You couldn't understand
My endless
Stream of tears
As you turned to walk away
But they weren't unleashed from your abrupt departure
They'd been building up for ages
Like a volcano
About to erupt
Suddenly free to flow
A force so disturbing
They could no longer be suppressed
Maybe your decision freed not just my volcanic tears,
But me as well.

Ashes

Ashes falling over the sea
You scattered them after you left the key
To the door, the life we shared, my heart
Though the flames were ablaze, my world went dark
You held my words, my passion, my soul
With the flick of a match, my chest has gone cold
With letters burned, charred fragments in the wind
You're free, and my sorrow shall have no end
Ashes fading into the sea
If I'm dead to you, I'm dead to me.

Stab Wounds

How you stab me
With your eyes
Telling me distance
Was never enough
To heal wounds

How you stab me
Digging the blade
Deeper
Forcing me
To pull the knife
From my own chest
So I can bury you
Again

I reapply the bandages
And wipe searing tears
From my face,
Indignantly curious
If you ever feel stab wounds
Or if you feel this ache.

Mural

I took the black and blue,
The darkest hues
The red that ran from our wounds,
I mixed them, swirled them
With the pale
And flung them across the room
They splattered the canvas
An explosion of colors
A chaotic outpouring of truth,
The wretched mixed in with the
Fairest of paints,
And no one would get it but you.

Old Song

Old song, how you sting
Like salty tears on a cut
I thought had healed so long ago
Assaulting me with memories
I left six feet under
Making me shudder
As if no time had ever passed
I rub the salt away
And turn the dial.

The Scent is Gone

The scent is gone
My pulse is slowing,
Without your fragrance
I just can't keep going

I buried my face
In the fabric, inhaled,
But there was nothing,
Just a memory so frail

If I can't hold on to this
Tangible piece,
How will I keep you
Alive, with me?

The scent is gone
My pulse is fading fast,
Your sweatshirt was the link
To make the memory of you last.

Weight

Had I known missing you
Would hurt this much,
I would have stayed
I would have forgotten about the rest,
And now this twenty-twenty
How it torments me
How it weighs upon my chest.

Ghosts

I see our ghosts arguing
On the cobblestone streets of Main,
Though our yelling fades into laughter
Still, I have to look away

On the banks of that murky river
Our ghosts dance in the light of day,
Unconcerned with the world around them
But I have to look away

I see them at night, looking at stars
Nestled close as the crickets play,
I know they're not real; they are only our ghosts,
But I can see them plain as day

I see our ghosts embracing
And I can't bear to look away,
They own every spec of this town
I have no choice; I can't stay.

Forgotten

I ran to the edge of the world
To forget your tortured expression last we met,
There were shadows plaguing your features
The marks of injury and regret

New lines swept from your eyes
No longer alive, but vacant and alone,
And underneath, circles so dark
The look of a person without a home

I ran to the edge of the world
To forget your tortured expression last we met,
But no matter how far the distance,
I haven't forgotten it yet.

Still Life

If I could paint a still life,
I would capture your photo inside,
Right next to the deck of cards
We used to play into the night

I'd paint your cotton t-shirt
The four by four you used to drive,
The notes and the letters you wrote
That got me through the darkest times

I'd paint the radio, your camera,
Your hand as it clung to mine,
Theater tickets, boot-cut jeans
Your arms holding me tight

If I could paint a still life,
I would capture you inside,
But I can't paint,
Yet the still life of us
Is imprinted on my mind.

Absence of You

The absence of you
Carved a hole in my chest,
Still aching
Despite the passing of time.
If I could talk to you now,
Fix my gaze on your face,
Or rest in your unwavering embrace,
I wouldn't let go,
I'd say I can't get through.
Nothing could've prepared me
For the absence of you.

I found Your Scarf

I found your scarf
It broke my last fragment of peace,
Tears welled up at once,
I collapsed to my knees

I crushed it in my grip
And pulled it to my face,
Searching for something tangible,
Even the slightest trace

It had to hold a piece of you,
It would bring you back again,
In the fibers of the wool,
I'd find your scent or feel your skin

Yet I came up empty,
But for tears falling anew,
If only you were here,
You'd tell me just what I should do

I found your scarf
It broke my last fragment of peace,
There's nothing in that fabric,
Just these haunting memories.

Imagine

I imagine you'll show up
You'll rescue me from the depths of despair,
I keep glancing over my shoulder
But I'm alone, you're never there

I wait for the sound of your steps
The faintest knock upon my door,
The passing of time plays games with my head
You couldn't possibly love me once more

I dream of the treble in your voice
I picture your face grinning back at me,
But awake to more heartache and tears
It's never real, only a dream

I imagine you will show up
You'll end this despair, you'll fix this mess,
But though I wait, I hope, I pray for the day
You're still gone, there's no sign of you yet.

Portrait

Your eyes awaken
As you study her,
She's a portrait
Come to life.
For your eyes to look
Upon me like that once more,
What I'd sacrifice.

Medicine

Where are you
When I need to lay
My head upon your chest,
To listen to your grounding beat
Thread my fingers around your neck

It unsettles me
How I need you still
In spite of all you've put me through,
Without your embrace,
My medicine
I don't know what to do

Come back,
I need to lay my head
Upon your healing chest,
To feel your arms as they hold me secure
Thread my fingers around your neck.

Paths

I saw a rusty pick-up truck
And willed it to be you,
Fate had crossed our paths again
In spite of everything we'd been through

I raced after the fading green
Panicking about which words to choose,
Time hadn't changed a thing
My heart was recklessly beating for you

I saw the rusty pick-up truck
And prayed my wish would come true,
If fate had given us another chance
I wouldn't let go of you.

III

Renewed

Sight

You had to leave
To look for answers
You were running towards the lights,
But in the end you discovered
All that you needed was here in plain sight

You had to leave
So you could realize
Life would never be perfect, just right,
But in the end you discovered
The things that mattered
Were here the whole time.

Demons

If I lock away my demons
And entrust you with the key,
Will you hold me as they try to take flight
As they battle for their release?

For if there are demons reigning over
The part of me I thought was free,
Then I'll willingly incarcerate them for you,
With you I'd rather be

If I lock away my demons
Things about me you hate to see,
As they try to break out,
As they beg for release,
Will you promise to hold on to me?

Itemized Scars

Why waste our breath
With more excuses
Or itemize our scars
Or place the blame,
When we can heal
The wounds we've inflicted
From this point on
With the love that remains

Why waste our tears
When we could save them
For bittersweet moments yet to come,
Love can heal the trauma we've inflicted
If we only let go,
We can surely move on.

Young At Heart

It's not only for the young,
The ravishing, or innocent,
Like the coins once lining our pockets
It's not gone; It's not spent.

We may not be as tender at heart
But sorrow has opened our eyes,
A love like that isn't just for them
We can have it; If only we try.

Rhythm

Let me dance to the rhythm of a music,
A song, my ears alone can hear,
Just allow me to be free for a time
Then you can draw me near

When I'm moving
Lost in the strum, unfiltered melody, the beat,
I can return to you unburdened
And love you purely, genuinely

Let me dance to the rhythm of a music
Chords, my ears alone can hear,
I'll come back with the love you crave
And a promise that you can draw me near.

Breath

You resuscitate my limbs
Fill my lungs with the sweetest breath,
When you were gone
My vitals slowed
Life was withering, hardly left

When you are near
I feel renewed
The pulse is fluid in my chest,
You resuscitate my being
You fill my lungs with the sweetest breath.

Your Song

I want to lose myself
In the treble of your voice
Feel your whispers along my neck,
Your words, your touch a symphony
Your song a sweet caress.

Float

They float across the quiet waters
Rays of sunshine warm their skin,
The breeze guides the tiny boat
Leaves rustling nearby sing their hymn

He holds her in his arms
Intertwined, they drift along,
Lazy smiles, two souls complete
Nothing, anywhere, could possibly be wrong.

Silence

I missed our comfortable silence
Relaxing, no plans
Content, no rush,
The glances without expectation
Genuine peace, the smiles, the hush

I missed our comfortable silence
Relaxing, no worries
No list, no rush,
But mostly I missed
Unspoken messages
Hidden in silence enveloping us.

Truer

Before,
Our mistakes, our endless trials
Were like scars we would always see,
A condemning record, a list of reasons
Our love could never be

But at some point we blinked
The veil rose, and we could suddenly see,
Our love had been tested, but fortified
And is now truer
Than we ever could have dreamed.

Savor

Savor me
Savor the scars
Savor the bumps along the road,
Savor the second that we met
Savor the highs; savor the lows

Take the flashbacks, precious and cruel
Learn to let the best ones play,
Savor the people we've become
Savor the triumphs along the way

Recall the bottom of the pit
How it felt to watch it all collapse,
Savor the mayhem we overcame
How we fought to get it back

Savor me
Savor you
Savor the bumps along the way,
Savor this second; we're still going strong
Savor the mistakes that made us change.

Unshakeable

We don't waste our time with regret
Though we once were so hurt and afraid,
We've accepted each other for who we really are
Clearly in the light of day

If it hadn't been for tribulation
We might not have seen anything worth the save,
We defied the odds, scaled cliffs, found forgiveness
And shielded our love from the grave

We don't waste our time with regret
We see the bond that grew from the pain,
We're imperfect, human, and utterly hopeless
But our love's unshakeable all the same.

Still See the You

I can still see the you who made my heart race
Who swept me off my feet,
When you reach for my hand, or give me a smile,
Or fix your gaze on me

Time can't touch the feeling inside
When my ear is to your chest,
Nothing could change the repose I feel here
No misstep, trial, or test

I can still see the you who makes my heart race
You still sweep me off my feet,
As you reach for my hand, give me a smile,
And fix your gaze on me.

Brokenness

She thought her brokenness would ravage his heart
It'd be better with them miles apart

He'd never look at her the same
Run his fingers down her face

She ran as far as she could go
The anguish nearly killed them both

But he refused to let her slip away
He rescued them; it wasn't too late

Her brokenness was his to share
An affliction he would gladly bear

As long as she was next to him
Her brokenness could not break them.

Run

Run away with me
For a few minutes
We'll kick off our shoes
And run for the shore,
Leave all of your quandaries
Behind you
Pretend we are smooth-skinned and audacious once more

Don't hesitate
When you reach the water
Just follow my lead
And jump right in,
We'll make a memory,
Though it may be fleeting
Moments like this, we'll treasure in the end.

Heartbeat

A drum, drowning out the rest
A heartbeat led me to you,
The passing of time has left it's mark
Certainly a scar or two

Just yesterday we were dancing to that cadence
Of the same incessant beat,
But age and trials have dealt their blows
And burdened us with defeat

Yet, that long ago tempo, I can sense it somehow
It's muffled, though not as strong,
The pulse of my heart still led me to you
And to you, I'll always belong.

A Note from the Author

Thank you for reading my new poetry collection. If you enjoyed *Absence of You*, I'd love for you to tell a friend or post a review on the site you purchased it from. I read every review and appreciate them all. Stay up-to-date with me on my Facebook page, Sarah Elle Emm, for upcoming book releases and extra poetry. Thanks for your continued love and enthusiasm.

~Sarah

Acknowledgements

To all of my family, friends, and readers, thank you for your support, reviews, and for sharing my work with others. May God bless you.

A special thank you to my cover designer, Natasha Brown, for her amazing work and vision. Thank you for the formatting and typesetting, Odyssey Books. Also, thank you to Brand Photo Design for the author photo.

I have to say thank you, especially to my mother, Jacque, for her extra set of editing eyes and her endless support and encouragement. You make me believe in myself…even when you remind me of how crazy I am. I would like to take this opportunity to point out that reading Stephen King while you were pregnant with me could have caused more damage than you realized. Ha, ha, ha. I love you!

To my dad, Mark, I am so grateful for your encouragement and love you more than I can say! I picture you singing, saying silly rhymes, and playing the drums sometimes when I'm in poetry mode. Thanks for the inspiration.

Coleen, my dear, dear sister…You are the best older sister ever, and thank you for the emergency supply of editing cookies and for the phone conversations that make me smile. I love you so much.

Sam Standring, the world's coolest brother, you are so kind to support your writer sister in all of my endeavors. Thanks for making me laugh. I love you.

To my husband, Charles, thanks for encouraging me to keep writing and to dream big. I love you!

To my beautiful daughters, Audrey and Sabrina, I just want to say thank you for always taking care of me. You are so smart, loving, and kind. I don't know what I'd do without you! Never forget...God loves you, and so do I!

About the Author

Sarah Elle Emm is the author of ABSENCE OF YOU, LAST VACATION, the HARMONY RUN SERIES, and MARRYING MISSY. An Indiana native and graduate of the University of Evansville, she has lived in Germany, England, Mexico, the U.S. Virgin Islands, and traveled extensively beyond. Sarah lives in the Outer Banks with her family. When she's not leading kitchen dance parties with her daughters, she writes poetry and fiction. Visit her website at SarahElleEmm.com. Follow her Facebook page, Sarah Elle Emm.

www.ingramcontent.com/pod-product-compliance
Lightning Source LLC
Chambersburg PA
CBHW020556030426
42337CB00013B/1110